Misery Births Ministry

30 Days of Grace, Faith, and Deeper Reflection with God

Myrian Menzie

Misery Births Ministry

Copyright © 2024 Myrian Menzie

Foreword

With great excitement, I write this foreword because it has been my pleasure watching Ms. Menzie grow into the woman she is today. For over 10 years, I've had the privilege to sow the word into her life, encourage her, and see God's anointing at work in her. I sincerely believe this book will show each reader the deep heart she has for God. It's especially for those who often feel left out. The anointing she carries is meant for this generation and those to coming, helping bring freedom in Christ through prayer and faith.

As you read through these pages, you'll find clarity to situations in life that often leave us wondering about our relationship with God and ourselves.

The personal stories and touching rhetoric, give us biblical context with testimonials that allow the reader to engage in the peace of knowing that God is always there with them. This is a Revelations 12:11 type of perspective, which guides us through how the blood of the lamb and our testimonies overcome us.

I can't wait to see how God will use this book to change lives and transform many hearts.

God Bless,

Pastor Joshua Williams Sr.

Youth Leader and Associate Pastor

WhiteHill M.B.C

Table of Contents

Introduction

After God placed it on my heart to write a book, I ignored it. Then God kept showing me signs and confirmation that this was one of his purposes for me. So then I kept telling God why I wasn't fit to write the book. And guess what! God kept telling me why I was fit to write the book.

When I finally said, "Okay, God, you have my yes," that was when the devil hit me like never before. I started battling with depression, anxiety, and suicidal thoughts. The night I wrote the most pages in my book, I had already decided that I was going to give up. I wrote a "suicide note". And when I finished, God said, "This book is going to save souls, and that's why the devil wants you dead." So, when I say I went through the worst years of my life, it's true. But that pressure—it's what created the diamond. My misery birthed my ministry.

Day 1

Shiloh

"And the peace of God, which transcends all understanding, will guard your hearts and your minds in Christ Jesus."

Reflection

I was driving, listening to *Cycles* by Jonathan McReynolds, when I began praying. I asked God to break every curse, stronghold, chain, and cycle in my life, and in the lives of everyone connected to me. As I went into worship, and the spirit of depression was on my mind because I felt that was a cycle I needed to break.

When I finished praying, something powerful happened. I saw 3 crosses and a sign that read *Shiloh*. So I started to look up the meaning, and it turned out to mean *"place or peace."*

Right then, I felt God speaking to me. I can say I know from experience God listens. He wanted me to know every Spirit, cycle, and stronghold was broken, and it was going to bring me and everyone connected to me to a place of peace!

Reflection Questions

- What cycles or strongholds do you feel you need to break?

- How has God shown you peace in challenging moments?

- Why do you think God's peace transcends understanding?

- How can worship and prayer help you address mental or spiritual battles?

- How do you remind yourself that God listens to your prayers?

Practical Exercise

Take 10 minutes today to write down any struggles or cycles you want to surrender to God. Pray over them and ask for His peace.

PERSONAL REFLECTION

"God's peace surpasses all understanding and guards my heart and mind."

(Answer the reflection questions here)

Day 2

Different problem, Same solver

"I the LORD do not change. So you, the descendants of Jacob, are not destroyed."

Reflection

I must admit, it's much easier to trust God when I can see he at least started doing what I asked him to do. Many times, I already have planned out in my head how God is going to do what I asked. But when He is not moving, how, when, or the way I map it out in my mind, I tend to lose faith. In the Word, He tells us that he is the same God, and he does NOT change. I learned to start looking at things that God has already done, and know that he is the same. If he was able to fix a situation just because the situation changed, it doesn't mean that God's power and ability to move mountains have changed.

Reflection Questions

- Can you recall a time when God resolved a situation differently than you expected?

- What does Malachi 3:6 reveal about God's unchanging nature?

- How can reflecting on God's past faithfulness strengthen your current faith?

- What areas of your life are hardest to trust God with?

- How can you practice trusting God's timing and plan?

Practical Exercise

Make a list of three situations where God has shown His faithfulness in the past. Keep this list as a reminder of His unchanging nature.

PERSONAL REFLECTION

"God does not change, and His power is always sufficient for my needs."

(Answer the reflection questions here)

Day 3

Rain

"Even though I walk through the darkest valley, I will fear no evil, for you are with me."

Reflection

I was driving and couldn't see it, so I prayed for God to stop the rain. He didn't stop it completely, but He made the eased the rain enough for me to see. A lot of times, we pray that God will remove "problems" from our lives, and we expect God to do just that. God can take the very problem, keep it there, and still allow us to fulfill our purpose. But sometimes, God doesn't promise to remove the valleys, but he said in his word that he will get in the valley with us! (Deuteronomy 31:6)

Reflection Questions

- How does Psalm 23:4 encourage you during difficult times?

- Have you experienced a time when God didn't remove a problem but gave you the strength to endure it?

- What does it mean to walk through the valley with God?

- How can you remind yourself of God's presence in challenging moments?

- What does "slacking the rain" symbolize in your life?

Practical Exercise

Reflect on a current "valley" in your life. Write down ways you've seen God's presence, even if the problem hasn't been removed.

PERSONAL REFLECTION

"God walks with me through every valley and gives me strength."

(Answer the reflection questions here)

Day 4

Intentional God

"For the pain you are feeling right now, cannot compare to your victory that is coming."

Reflection

I was so angry with my mother for many years. She was a youth leader at our church, and I would always hear about how much she helped others. I was angry because I felt because she was helping everyone else, she did not realize her own child was battling with depression and suicidal thoughts. This was not the case. She did not realize that God needed me alone so that I would know HE is always there. A lot of times, we blame others, when everything that happens has to get past God first. If he allowed it, there is a reason why.

Reflection Questions

- How can hardships draw you closer to God?

- Why is it important to trust that God allows things for a purpose?

- How has God used solitude in your life to teach you about His presence?

- What does Romans 8:18 teach about enduring pain for future glory?

- How can you release blame and trust God's plan?

Practical Exercise

Write a letter to God expressing your feelings about a current challenge and asking Him to reveal His purpose in it.

PERSONAL REFLECTION

"God uses every situation for His purpose and my good."

(Answer the reflection questions here)

Day 5

God's Eyes

"Fearfully and Wonderfully made 'I praise you because I am fearfully and wonderfully made; your works are wonderful, I know that full well.'"

Reflection

I would always get compliments on the very things I hated the most about me. I changed my prayer to God: help me to see me how you see me. The things that God finds so beautiful and unique about us, sometimes we don't see the beauty in his creativity because we are not seeing ourselves how God sees us.

Reflection Questions

- What do you dislike about yourself that others often compliment?

- How can you start seeing yourself as God sees you?

- What does it mean to be fearfully and wonderfully made?

- How can focusing on God's creativity change your perspective on self-image?

- How does embracing your uniqueness glorify God?

Practical Exercise

Look in the mirror and thank God for three specific traits you have, acknowledging His handiwork in creating you.

PERSONAL REFLECTION

"I am fearfully and wonderfully made in God's image."

(Answer the reflection questions here)

Day 6

God Says

"For I know the plans I have for you, 'declares the Lord,' plans to prosper you and not to harm you, plans to give you hope and a future."

Reflection

Waiting on an answer from God is much like playing, Simon says. You're just sitting there waiting and anticipating if it is going to be God saying yes or if it is going to be God saying no. I was on my bathroom floor crying, waiting for an answer from God. And God didn't give me the answer I was anticipating he would say. It wasn't what I wanted, but it was what I needed. It may hurt when you don't get the answer you want. It may even cost you some things, but the pain is only temporary. God sees all, and he knows all. He knows what is ahead, so trust what God says.

Reflection Questions

- How do I feel about changes in my life?
- In what ways can faith help me embrace new seasons?
- What changes have I resisted, and why?
- How have past changes contributed to my growth?
- What's one way I can trust God's guidance today?

Practical Exercise

Write down one change you fear and brainstorm a small step you can take to face it with faith.

PERSONAL REFLECTION

"Today, I trust that change is part of God's plan for my growth."

(Answer the reflection questions here)

Day 7

Give it to God

"The least of you will become a thousand, the smallest a mighty nation. I am the Lord; in its time I will do this swiftly."

Reflection

I was doing my statistics homework, and I couldn't seem to get the material. I decided to take a break and come back to it. When I couldn't get it, I just decided it was too late. I felt there wasn't enough time for me to work out the problems and enter the answer. I put up my notebook, closed my computer, and said I was forgetting I had prayed to understand and get it done. I said well, let me try what I can. Let's skip to the good part. I finished with 100% four minutes before the due date. I allowed the circumstances I was in to allow me to forget the ability and power that the God that I serve has.

Reflection Questions

- What uncertainties are weighing on me today?

- How can I find peace without having all the answers?

- Who can I reach out to for encouragement?

- How does trusting God help in times of doubt?

- What does "peace" look like for me today?

Practical Exercise

Spend at least 10 minutes in quiet prayer or meditation, focusing on breathing and releasing worry.

PERSONAL REFLECTION

"Today, I find peace in trusting that God holds my future."

(Answer the reflection questions here)

Day 8

Focus

"fixing our eyes on Jesus, the pioneer and perfecter of faith. For the joy set before him he endured the cross, scorning its shame, and sat down at the right hand of the throne of God."

Reflection

The reason why I get so afraid of driving is because of others around me. Even though I know the speed limit, if others are going at a fast pace, I feel the need to speed up. If others are driving super slow, I start going slow because they obviously know something I don't. I had to learn that it's not about how others around me drive as long as I obey the rules of the road. The promises and rules of life are all in the Bible. It's important not to get distracted by what others are doing around you. Do what God tells you!

Reflection Questions

- Who in my life could use encouragement?

- How does serving others enrich my faith?

- When have I felt joy in helping someone?

- What small act of kindness can I do today?

- How can serving others bring me closer to God?

Practical Exercise

Perform a small act of kindness for someone, whether a family member, friend, or stranger.

PERSONAL REFLECTION

"Today, I find joy in serving others as a reflection of God's love."

(Answer the reflection questions here)

Day 9

Resist

"Submit yourselves, then, to God. Resist the devil, and he will flee from you."

Reflection

I was talking to God about something I knew wasn't pleasing to him. I told him I wasn't sure if I could stop. Then he put the scripture on my heart to resist the devil, and he will flee. As I was on my way to work, I was reading my verse of the day, and that was the verse of the day. 7 So give yourselves to God. Stand against the devil, and he will run away from you. (

Reflection Questions

- Who do I need to forgive, and why?

- How does holding onto bitterness affect me?

- What steps can I take toward forgiving others?

- How can I practice self-forgiveness?

- How does forgiveness help me grow spiritually?

Practical Exercise

Write a letter of forgiveness to someone (you don't have to send it). Focus on letting go of the hurt.

PERSONAL REFLECTION

"Today, I release bitterness and embrace forgiveness for healing."

(Answer the reflection questions here)

Day 10

Confirmation

"He says, 'Be still, and know that I am God; I will be exalted among the nations, I will be exalted in the earth.'"

Reflection

I mentioned before in the book that I battled with Suicidal thoughts once I gave God my yes. My family joined together to visit my uncle's church for my niece's christening three days after I wrote my suicidal letter. When I finished, God told me that I would live!! We went through service, and the church was great. When my uncle gave his topic, it was "You can't kill what God has anointed to live." I always joke and say God is telling my business. He definitely told my uncle about my business. He began preaching and started talking about Suicide in our generation. I thank God that he reminds us that he is listening. I thank God that when we are anointed, there is nothing that the devil can do to kill us.

Reflection Questions

- When have I felt God speaking to me?

- How can I quiet distractions to hear God's guidance?

- What does it mean to listen with an open heart?

- How might God be speaking to me today?

29

- How does listening deepen my relationship with God?

Practical Exercise

Take 10 minutes in quiet reflection, letting God speak to you through your thoughts, feelings, or scripture.

PERSONAL REFLECTION

"Today, I open my heart to hear God's voice in stillness."

(Answer the reflection questions here)

Day 11

Liberty

"Now the Lord is the Spirit, and where the Spirit of the Lord is, there is freedom."

Reflection

I had a customer one day that was absolutely rude. My flesh wanted to return the same attitude. But I reminded myself not to let her change me, but it seemed after I told myself that she became even more hateful. I finally decided the devil wouldn't win. I prayed, "God, give her a heart like you." Her entire attitude changed. She thanked me for helping her, and she even told me to have a good day. Sometimes, we allow flesh to win. We have to remember that where the spirit of the Lord is, there is liberty. And that means we can be free from ANYTHING!

Reflection Questions

- What role does prayer play in my daily routine?

- Where can I make space for quiet moments with God each day?

- What daily habits either draw me closer to or distance me from my faith?

- How often do I pause to listen for God's guidance?

- How can my actions today reflect God's love for those around me?

Practical Exercise

Identify one habit in your routine that could use a positive adjustment and commit to making that change today.

PERSONAL REFLECTION

"I made a small change to grow closer to God."

(Answer the reflection questions here)

Day 12

God's speed

"Jesus replied, 'You do not realize now what I am doing, but later you will understand.'"

Reflection

When I was growing up, my mom's washer would take about 15-20 minutes to complete a load of clothes. When I moved to my own place, I couldn't understand why mine took over an hour. Did it mean one was a better wash than the other? God spoke to me. He said every time you get discouraged looking at others your age and their path, think of this. Just because you are at different speeds, does not mean work is not being done in and through you. Some take longer; some take shorter. The end result is the same!

Reflection Questions

- When have I experienced grace from others in unexpected ways?

- How do I feel when I forgive or extend grace to someone else?

- What's one area where I could show myself more grace?

- In what ways have I seen God's grace at work in my life recently?

- Who in my life could use grace instead of judgment today?

Practical Exercise

Extend grace to someone today, offering forgiveness or understanding instead of criticism.

PERSONAL REFLECTION

"Today, I chose grace over judgment."

(Answer the reflection questions here)

Day 13

You may bend, but you won't break

"But as for you, be strong and do not give up, for your work will be rewarded."

Reflection

I was in worship crying out to God, asking Him for a sign. I wanted to know that everything was going to be okay. I sat for hours crying out, praying, worshiping. It wasn't until the next day that I realized what was right in front of me. I was staring right at bamboo. I instantly thought about the significance of the rapid growth of bamboo, but God said that is not what I need you to see now. I began to research. God revealed to me that bamboo was significant because of their endurance during the storm. The bend with the wind. After the storm, they stand tall. He let me, though even though I may bend, I will not break. When the storm ends, I will still stand tall. My posture of praise after the storm is what draws others near Him.

Reflection Questions

- How can I bring peace into my own heart before sharing it with others?

- Are there relationships in my life that need healing or peace?

- How does active listening contribute to peaceful interactions?

- Who in my life brings a sense of peace, and how do they do it?

- What can I let go of to make more room for peace?

Practical Exercise

Take some time today to listen actively to someone without interrupting or planning your response.

PERSONAL REFLECTION

"I listened patiently to encourage peace."

(Answer the reflection questions here)

Day 14

Give it over

"Cast all your anxiety on him because he cares for you."

Reflection

I was crying out to God about how tired I was of fighting. God immediately spoke to me. When I was younger, I would go with my friend to her track meets. My favorite was the relay race. God said just like the relay race, you are tired because you have not passed the baton. Just like in the relay race, that person is only trained to run a certain distance. After they have run their distance, they must trust their partner to finish the race. He said you have done all you can do. It's time to cast it unto me. Until you let it go, he can not pick it up.

Reflection Questions

- What situations cause me to feel lost or uncertain?

- How do I feel after praying in times of uncertainty?

- When was a time that prayer brought me peace and clarity?

- How often do I rely on my own strength instead of turning to God?

- What would it look like to make prayer a natural response to stress?

Practical Exercise

Set aside five minutes to pray for clarity and peace about something that's weighing on your heart.

PERSONAL REFLECTION

"I took time to pray for peace and direction."

(Answer the reflection questions here)

Day 15

All knowing God

"Nothing in all creation is hidden from God's sight. Everything is uncovered and laid bare before the eyes of him to whom we must give account."

Reflection

I was talking with my mom about how I battle with low self-esteem. One day, I felt so ugly. This day happened to be my cousin's college graduation. On the inside, I felt so down, but I had to pretend for everyone else. As we were out celebrating, a young girl stopped me to tell me I was so beautiful. Although she didn't know I needed that, God did. He knows exactly what we need. We can't hide from Him. He reminds us he hears. He sees. He cares. He loves us. We are his creation. Everything he made is good.

Reflection Questions

- Who in my life needs encouragement or support today?
- How does sharing kindness or encouragement impact my own heart?
- When have I felt God's light shine through others during my hard times?
- What qualities do I appreciate most in people who bring light to others?
- How can I share God's light in a simple, practical way today?

Practical Exerci

Send an encoura   note, text, or call to someone who could use a
reminder that the   not alone.

PERSONAL REFLECTION

"I believe that God is all-knowing and nothing works without His allowing it."

(Answer the reflection questions here)

Day 16

Perfect Timing

"There is a time everything, and a season for every activity under the heaven

Reflection

As I was traveling here was a car behind me that was driving above the speed t. This caused me to drive faster, when I already knew the ed limit of the road. Just because somebody else is going at a erent speed or a different rate than you doesn't mean that you ne o change your speed. God gives us different journeys. We can allow the enemy to distract us into thinking someone else's p is ours. We must ask our will to align with God's perfect wi r our life.

Reflection Ques is

- How hav u experienced God's perfect timing in your life?

- What are f your life require patience and trust in God's timing?

- When have you tried to rush God's process, and what was the outcome?

- How can recognizing God's timing help you align your plans with His?

- What does "perfect timing" mean to you personally?

Practical Exercise

Reflect on a current situation where you're struggling with timing. Write down your feelings about it and pray for patience and trust in God's perfect timing.

PERSONAL REFLECTION

"Today, I trust God's timing is perfect and His plans for me are unfolding beautifully."

(Answer the reflection questions here)

Day 17

Omnipresent God

"Be strong and courageous. Do not be afraid or terrified because of them, for the Lord your God goes with you; he will never leave you nor forsake you."

Reflection

One day, I was traveling, and I received a notification, "We have found a safer route because the route you are on has severe thunderstorm warnings. I immediately went into a panic. I had no idea there was supposed to be a storm. I began to ask God what to do. I was only comfortable driving the way I was headed. However, I was not comfortable driving through storms. I prayed. God spoke instantly. He told me to continue on the route I was already headed for. I did not need a safer route because the route I was on was safe enough. He is able to keep me no matter where I am. During the remaining time, it didn't rain a drop. The sky was beautiful. The sun shined on me so bright. The Son shined through me.

Reflection Questions

- What fears have you been struggling with lately, and how have they affected your decisions?

- When fac   with fear, how does your faith in God bring
  you comf   and courage?
- Why is it   ortant to trust God even when outcomes seem
  uncertain
- What exa   es from Scripture inspire you to choose faith
  over fear
- What is o   step you can take today to confront a fear with
  faith?

Practical Exerci

Identify a fear yo   e been avoiding. Spend time in prayer, asking
God for courage   guidance to face it. Take one small step of
faith toward ove   ning it today.

PERSONAL REFLECTION

"Today, I choose to trust in God's power over my fears."

(Answer the reflection questions here)

Day 18

What you need is only hidden

"I will give you hidden treasures, riches stored in secret places, so that you may know that I am the Lord, the God of Israel, who summons you by name."

Reflection

My grandparents have always been a great help to everyone. They are willing to give their last to anyone. They never ask for anything in return. I went to stay with them for the weekend. This particular weekend, they poured so much into me. I don't think they realized how much I needed them. It was on my heart to sow a seed into them. I knew they wouldn't take a token of love from me, so I hid it until I left town. When I got home, my grandfather called to let me know I had forgotten something. I let them know that it was a gift to them. He said no, you didn't have to. A lot of time, God has things for us. It does not mean we won't receive it. If he gives it to us at the wrong time, we may send it back. Don't be misled; what you need is just hidden right now.

Reflection Questions

- In what areas of your life do you feel weak or inadequate?

- How does acknowledging your weakness open the door for God's strength?

- What does it mean for God's power to be made perfect in your weakness?

- Have you experienced a time when God's strength carried you through a tough season?

- How can you share your testimony of strength and weakness to encourage others?

Practical Exercise

Write down a current struggle where you feel weak. Then, write a prayer inviting God to show His strength in that area. Carry this prayer with you as a reminder throughout the day.

ERSONAL REFLECTION

"God's streng   ines brightest in my moments of weakness."

(A   ver the reflection questions here)

Day 19

Obedience is better than sacrifice

"In the same way, the Spirit helps us in our weakness. We do not know what we ought to pray for, but the Spirit himself intercedes for us through wordless groans."

Reflection

I was driving for a long distance. It was one of the days I was extremely tired. Normally, I pray before cranking my car, but it was one of those days. While almost twelve miles from my destination, I realized I didn't pray. I began to pray even though I was close. As soon as I said amen, a car made a U-turn right in front of me. Going at a high rate of speed, I had to slam on my brakes. I was able to stop with no crash. I immediately thanked God. When you get the urge to pray, pray. If you don't know what to pray, start calling on Jesus. The spirit makes intercession for us. We just have to be obedient.

Reflection Questions

- Have you ever felt prompted to pray but ignored it? What was the outcome?
- How does Romans 8:26 encourage you when you're unsure of what to pray for?
- Why do you think obedience to God's prompting is more important than doing things your own way?

56

- When ha_ ou experienced God's protection or guidance because o _ur obedience?
- How can _ make prayer a more consistent part of your daily rout _ ?

Practical Exerci

Take five minute _ day to pray, even if you're not sure what to say. Let the Holy _ irit guide you, or just call on Jesus. Afterward, take a moment to _ lect on how it felt, and write down any thoughts or insig _ that came to you.

PERSONAL REFLECTION

"My words carry the power to bless, heal, and encourage."

(Answer the reflection questions here)

Day 20

Listen

Reflection

I started my mas   ; program after being out of school for two
years. It was ver   st-paced, and I was struggling to get back in
the swing of thin   At the same time, I was juggling a job. I
missed the due d   for my first assignment. I began to panic. God
told me to submi   e assignment anyway. Of course, I wanted to
talk back like Gc   oes not know everything. I'm like, God, it's
too late, but I co   ted it and submitted it. When I submitted it, I
gave God thanks   ter, I was at TikTok mining, and I received an
email. The email   s that I received a perfect score on the
assignment. We   iot argue with God. We just have trust.
Everything is in   control.

Reflection Ques   is

- What situ   ins in your life are calling for trust in God's
  timing?

- How can   better listen for God's guidance in stressful
  moments

59

- Why is it important to follow God's lead, even when it doesn't make sense?

- How has God shown you that He is in control when you feel unsure?

- How can gratitude shape your response to God's unexpected blessings?

Practical Exercise

Reflect on a time when you hesitated to follow God's direction. Write about what happened and how trusting Him could have changed the outcome. Pray for clarity and courage to listen to Him in future situations.

ERSONAL REFLECTION

"Today,   ioose a heart of humility and service."

(A   ver the reflection questions here)

Day 21

Freedom looks good on you

"Do not conform to the pattern of this world, but be transformed by the renewing of your mind. Then you will be able to test and approve what God's will is—his good, pleasing and perfect will."

Reflection

We were able to represent our favorite college team for church. I could not decide on my past or current school. God spoke to me instantly. When I run into people, they always ask if I am still at Ole Miss. I immediately feel like I graduated years ago. The reason why people don't know we have come out of situations is because we still wear it on us. We wear the brokenness, bitterness, hurt, and shame. When God frees you, wear the freedom.

Reflection Questions

- What old patterns or labels are you still carrying that God has already freed you from?

- How does freedom in Christ transform how you see yourself?

- Why do we sometimes cling to our past, even when God offers renewal?

- Who in y　life could benefit from seeing your freedom in Christ?

- How can　reflect God's transformative power through your wor　nd actions?

Practical Exerci

Take a moment t　flect on what God has freed you from. Write a short declaration　rayer thanking Him for this freedom. Commit to walking confi　ly in His grace.

PERSONAL REFLECTION

"I am no longer bound by my past; I wear the freedom Christ has given me."

(Answer the reflection questions here)

Day 22

H₍ ₃ just doing his job

*"The thief comes ly to steal and kill and destroy; I have come
that they may ha fe, and have it to the full."*

Reflection

My fiancé and I e having trouble all morning. I had been up
since 4 am tossin nd turning. I had a migraine that just would not
go away. We cou 't see eye to eye. It just seemed nothing was
going right. I wa set, angry, and hurting. Out of nowhere, peace
came over me. I t into the house to see him crying. I
immediately thou the worst. I went to comfort him. He handed
me his phone. O₁ phone was an email. The email was
something we ha en praying about for over a year. Whenever
the enemy is con in every direction, I learned to praise. He
wants you to dist you from the direction you are headed in.
Your destination reakthrough, healing, peace, and joy.

Reflection Ques is

- How do y recognize when the enemy is trying to distract
  you?

- What too as God given you to combat spiritual attacks?

- How can praise shift your perspective during difficult moments?

- When has God turned a trial into a breakthrough for you?

- Why is it important to stay focused on God's promises, even in chaos?

Practical Exercise

Next time you feel under attack spiritually, stop and praise God. Write down a few specific promises from Scripture to declare over your situation.

PERSONAL REFLECTION

"Even when life hard, I'll choose to praise God and trust His plan."

(Answer the reflection questions here)

Day 23

Use your gift

"We have different gifts, according to the grace given to each of us. If your gift is prophesying, then prophesy in accordance with your faith; if it is serving, then serve; if it is teaching, then teach; if it is to encourage, then give encouragement; if it is giving, then give generously; if it is to lead, do it diligently; if it is to show mercy, do it cheerfully."

Reflection

At my brother's game, they have songs that they use to walk out to the plate. As my brother was walking out, I noticed he was the only one with a gospel song. This touched me so much. So many people thought my brother spent too much time on the baseball field. No one heard my brother pray like we heard my brother pray. No one knew how my brother had a relationship like he knew he had a personal relationship with God. Everything is not for show, but it is for God to get the glory. Whatever you do, use your gift to give God glory.

Reflection Questions

- What are some of the unique talents or gifts God has given you?

- How are you using those gifts to serve others?

- Why is it ᵘortant to use your gifts, even when no one is watching

- Can you ᵗ k of a time when you used your gifts to help someone ᵕ?

- How can ᵗ remind yourself that everything you do is for God's glᵒ

Practical Exerci

Take a moment tᵗ ink about how you can use your gifts this week, even in sm ways. Whether it's helping someone or encouraging thex ke action and see how God can use you.

PERSONAL REFLECTION

"My gifts are from God, and I will use them to honor Him."

(Answer the reflection questions here)

Day 24

He is the Son

"He says, "Be s͓   ͓nd know that I am God; I will be exalted among the natio͓   ͓ will be exalted in the earth."

Reflection

I was sitting wit͓   ͓ grandparents, letting them know that I was having a hard ti͓   ͓tting go. I have always been set apart, so when I find a "fr͓   ͓," sometimes I stay too long. I don't know when my season ͓   ͓p. My grandfather let me finish the conversation. Th͓   ͓ening went by. My granddad casually mentioned it wo͓   ͓e time to plant more vegetables in the garden soon. He said he ͓   ͓ted me to go with him. I said, " I would love to." He told me ͓   ͓anted me to throw the seeds out. He said that once you throw ͓   ͓eeds out, that's all you can do. When God gives us an assig͓   ͓nt, it is just for us to plant the seed. He does the watering. He ͓   ͓he son. He handles the rest.

Reflection Ques͓   ͓s

- What are ͓   ͓e areas in your life where you find it hard to let go?

- How do ͓   ͓ feel when you have to leave things behind or move on͓

- In what ways has God asked you to plant seeds and trust Him with the results?

- How does trusting God's timing give you peace in your own life?

- What "seeds" can you plant today, knowing that God will take care of the rest?

Practical Exercise

Think about something you're holding onto that you need to release. Pray and ask God to help you trust Him with it, knowing that He's in control of the outcome.

PERSONAL REFLECTION

"God plants the seeds, and He takes care of the rest."

(Answer the reflection questions here)

Day 25

Fisherman of Men

"Come, follow me," Jesus said, "and I will send you out to fish for people."

Reflection

My grandfather loves fishing. When he retired, he decided to fish full-time. I always complained about how my grandfather only took the boys fishing. I felt like he thought I was girly. Honestly, I was a little jealous. And yes, I know envy is not of God. God spoke to me. Many evenings, my granddad and I sit in the living room, and we read the bible, and we talk about the Word of God. Just because I was not in the lake catching the animals, I was still fishing. Since I was young, I've been fishing with my grandfather. My grandfather helped prepare me to be a fisherman of men.

Reflection Questions

- How has God used people in your life to shape you or teach you?

- In what ways can you be a "fisher of men" in your own life?

- Do you feel like your role in spreading God's love is important, even if it's not visible to others?

- How do y   share your faith with others, even when you don't thir   ou're "doing enough"?

- Who are   people in your life that need to experience God's lov   rough you?

Practical Exerc

Think about som   e you can reach out to today—whether through a kind w   , prayer, or sharing a scripture. Make a small, intentional effort   'fish for people" today.

PERSONAL REFLECTION

"God calls me to fish for people, and I will trust Him with the outcome."

(Answer the reflection questions here)

Day 26

Change your mindset

*"Do not conform   the pattern of this world, but be transformed
by the renewing   our mind. Then you will be able to test and
approve what Go   will is—his good, pleasing and perfect will."*

Reflection

I had a customer   day that was absolutely rude. My flesh
wanted to return   same attitude. I told myself not to let her
change me, but i   med after I told myself that she became even
more hateful. I fi   y decided the devil wouldn't win. I prayed,
"God, give her a   rt like you." Her entire attitude changed. She
thanked me for h   ng her, and she even told me to have a good
day. Sometimes,   allow flesh to win. We have to remember that
where the spirit   e Lord is, there is liberty. This means we can
be free from AN   HING!

Reflection Questions

- When wa   e last time you faced a difficult person or
  situation   responded with grace?

- How do y   normally handle conflicts or negative
  attitudes?

- How can changing your mindset help you respond more like Christ?

- What do you think it means to be "free" in Christ in every situation?

- How does choosing God's way of thinking lead to peace and freedom?

Practical Exercise

When you face a challenge or difficult person today, pause and ask God to help you see things from His perspective. Pray for His strength to respond with grace.

PERSONAL REFLECTION

"Where the Spirit the Lord is, there is freedom. I choose His way today."

(Answer the reflection questions here)

Day 27

Worth the wait

"For like the grass they will soon wither, like green plants they will soon die away. Take delight in the Lord, and he will give you the desires of your heart."

Reflection

For my college graduation, I was blessed with a car. When I went searching for a car, I knew exactly what I wanted. I wanted a white exterior. I wanted a brand new 2022. I really wanted leather seats. I wanted a sunroof. I went to a test drive at a car lot, where I was told I would not be able to get exactly what I wanted. I would have to settle. I told her I serve a God where I don't have to settle. I said that, but I still almost settled three times after that. I kept being patient and praying. A month after praying and waiting, my car was shipped in. It was a brand new 2022 Toyota rav4. It was white with a black leather interior. It definitely had a sunroof. It even had extra that I didn't pray about. With God, we can be confident. We can be arrogant. We don't have to limit God.

Reflection Questions

- What is something you've had to wait for in your life that turned out better than expected?
- How do you feel about waiting on God's timing?

- What are ͏ ͏e ways you can trust that God's plan is better than your ͏ n?
- How doe͏ ͏ ͏tience help you grow in your relationship with God?
- How can ͏ encourage someone else who is waiting on God's pe͏ ͏ t timing?

Practical Exerc͏

Think about a sit ͏ on where you are currently waiting. Write down the desires ͏ your heart and trust God to fulfill them in His perfect timing.

PERSONAL REFLECTION

"God's timing is perfect, and I will wait patiently for His best."

(Answer the reflection questions here)

Day 28

You're Enough

"A generous per   will prosper; whoever refreshes others will be refreshed."

Reflection

My grandmother   ⁄ays mentions how she does not have much. However, she ha   much. She has so much because she gives what she has. Sh   ways tells my cousins and I, "The Lord is my shepherd; I shall   want." My cousins and I have carried that. Most of us have   ast graduated from high school. We have been able to know thro   1 it all that we do not lack. We do not have to think we do not l   anything to share with others. God uses us all in different ways   are what you have with others.

Reflection Ques   1s

- What are   1e ways you've felt "not enough" in your life?

- How do y   see God's provision in your life, even when you feel l   you have little to give?

- How can   practice generosity, even when you feel like you don'   ve much?

- What doe   mean to you to be "enough" in God's eyes?

- How can you share what you have, no matter how small it seems, to bless others?

Practical Exercise

Today, take the time to give something to someone in need. It could be time, a kind word, or a small gift. Practice generosity and trust God to use it for His glory.

PERSONAL REFLECTION

"I have everything I need in Christ. I am enough."

(Answer the reflection questions here)

Day 29

Being a model for Christ

"Therefore, I urge you, brothers and sisters, in view of God's mercy, to offer your bodies as a living sacrifice, holy and pleasing to God—this is your true and proper worship."

Reflection

I kept hearing the word model. I walked into work, and my coworker was like, "You came here to model." I've never considered myself a model since I am very shy. I went to church, and someone said, "Look at this model." So I began to ask God. "What are you speaking to me?" My pastor then spoke about the model prayer. After church, I researched the word "model" and learned that a model shows you the representation of what something should look like. God told me He needs me to be a model for him, how I walk with Him, how I dress, how I present myself, and how I praise Him in the midst of it all. I was sitting in church the same day with thoughts of giving up. Yes, on the same day, everyone thought I was glowing. I noticed there was a little girl staring at me, and she waved. I knew I had to be a model for those watching.

Reflection Questions

- How do you feel about being a role model for others?
- In what ways can your actions reflect Christ to the people around you?

- What doe   mean to offer your body as a living sacrifice?
- How doe: ing a model for Christ influence the way you
live?
- Can you   k of someone who looks up to you? How can
you set a   lly example for them?

Practical Exerci

This week, be in   ional about how you live out your faith. Think
about how you c: nodel Christ's love in everyday situations.
Pray for God's h   to be a good example.

PERSONAL REFLECTION

"I will be a model for Christ in everything I do."

(Answer the reflection questions here)

Day 30

[e gets the glory

"And we know t/   n all things God works for the good of those
who love him, w/   ave been called according to his purpose."

Reflection

My oldest cousir   nt through trials while in college. His path did
not go the way h   nted it to. We actually ended up at college at
the same time. W ere able to spend time together and talk more.
My time came ar d when school didn't go as I planned. I
remembered that matter how he started, he was still finished.
So, I kept going. at you are going through, is not always just for
you. Somebody (needs to see God carry you through. Someone
needs to see it's   h it to hang in there.

Reflection Ques   ıs

- How have ıu seen God work through your struggles?
- How does owing that God is working everything for
  good cha your perspective on life's challenges?
- How can ı point others to God's glory, even when things
  are tough
- When you ok back on your life, what do you want people
  to see as greatest testimony of God's goodness?
- How can ı trust God to get the glory in every situation
  you face?

Practical Exercise

Think about a current challenge you're facing. Ask God to use it for His glory. Write down any insights you receive and share them with someone who might be encouraged by your story.

PERSONAL REFLECTION

"God gets the glory in all things, and I trust Him with every part of my journey."

(Answer the reflection questions here)

Prayer for Unbelief

God, thank You for being the Creator of everything around us.

I'm grateful that nothing happens without Your permission.

I ask for encouragement, not just for me, but for everyone I'm connected to.

Help us to remember the miracles You've already worked in our lives and give us the strength to trust You even more.

When we struggle with doubt, please help us in our unbelief.

Remind us that if You've done it once, You are more than able to do it again.

In Jesus Name.

Amen!

A Prayer for Freedom

Dear God,

Thank you for revealing Your promises to us at work.

I pray for anyone in bondage to be loose, no matter what that bondage may be for them.

You said in your Word that where the spirit of the Lord is, there is liberty.

So, Lord, I ask you rest in the minds, hearts, and souls of me and the people connected to me so we can experience the freedom you have already promised us.

In Jesus' name.

Amen.

A Prayer for Peace

God, thank You for unspeakable peace.

Thank You for giving us peace, even in the midst of situations that cause us and everyone around us to wonder how.

God, I pray in the name of Jesus that you cause every storm in my life and the lives of the people connected to it to cease.

I ask that every attack of the enemy that wants to cause disruption and commotion be stopped.

In the Name of Jesus.

Amen.

A Prayer for Strength

God, thank you for being my strength when I am weak.

I'm grateful that when I feel I have no strength to carry on, you will pick me up.

Thank You, Lord for not only allowing me to come to you with my burdens but also taking the load off of me.

I pray for strength in the name of Jesus in every area that I am weak in.

Please continue to uphold me in the midst of it all.

I speak your strength over me and everyone connected to me, for there is no one more powerful than you.

Made in the USA
Columbia, SC
25 November 2024

47234813R00057